Blossom
EDUCATIONAL
PUBLISHING

www.blossomhomeeducation.co.uk

Follow us on social media:

www.facebook.com/blossomhomeeducation

www.instagram.com/blossomhomeed

www.instagram.com/blossom_educational_publishing

www.twitter.com/blossom_homeed

Join our friendly group for parents:

www.facebook.com/blossomeducationalsupport

The Maths Curriculum for Parents

YEAR 1

By Katie J Browne

Contents

Introduction

This book is for any parent who wants to understand the National Curriculum maths objectives for Year 1 and is looking for practical ways to support their child's development in this area.

As a parent and a teacher myself, I hear first hand from many parents wanting to support their child's maths development but feeling underconfident with the demands of the current curriculum. There are countless products on the market to help, but not knowing which to buy can be both expensive and overwhelming. My aim is to create books that guide families through the curriculum, simply and without pressure.

Thank you for investing in this book. I really hope it helps you to support your child through their early maths development and would love to hear how you get on.

Katie

How to Use This Book

The objectives in this book have been broken up into eight sections:

- Place Value
- Addition and Subtraction
- Multiplication and Division
- Fractions
- Measurement
- Geometry: Shapes and Properties
- Geometry: Position and Direction

Each section contains multiple objectives, each with explanations, ideas and key vocabulary. Although separated within this book, many objectives will link strongly with others.

Structuring Your Approach

Parents who home educate and those with children at school might choose to approach these objectives in different ways. Either way, many of the objectives relate to each other and are strongly linked, so shouldn't simply be taught in the order they've been written. A child's understanding of place value forms a basis for most other areas of mathematics, so it is crucial to teach these skills both explicitly and alongside other areas throughout the year.

Children at school will be taught these objectives in the order chosen by their school. It might be a good idea to ask their teacher for a long term plan, so you can support your child on the objectives in line with their classroom learning. Alternatively, you could choose objectives by activity, in similar ways as suggested below.

If you home educate your child, there are many ways to fit these objectives into your routine. Some home educating families like to structure their week more formally, focusing on maths for a set period of time each day. If that is the case for your family, a long term plan like those used in schools could be an option. An example can be found here: www.whiterosemaths.com/resources/primary-resources/primary-sols/. This plan allows for a logical progression through the objectives, as well as repetition for consolidation and advancement. The order can be varied, but it is always a good idea to start with place value.

For families who take a more fluid, flexible approach to mathematics, this book provides many ideas for relating the National Curriculum objectives to real life situations and activities your child will enjoy. In this case, it could be useful to look through the entire book when you buy it, to get an idea of the different areas of mathematics to cover. When planning an activity, look though the book to see how it can relate to the curriculum. For example, if you are cooking with your child you might look at the measurement unit to familiarise yourself with the types of language to use with your child. As mentioned several times already, a good understanding of place value forms the foundations of your child's mathematical development. Read through this section and consider how the various objectives and activities could fit into your daily routines.

It might be useful to annotate the book or keep a notebook, making notes on any particular difficulties your child has faced when approaching these objectives, so that you know to spend longer on particular activities. Similarly, it is great to keep a record of your child's strengths, to extend them in these areas.

Key Vocabulary

Each unit includes at least one box of key vocabulary. This is language suggested for assisting, extending and assessing your child's understanding. It is not compulsory and you shouldn't worry if your child isn't able to use every word suggested in this book. Use this language yourself when working with your child to model how to use it. Children's language skills still vary greatly at this age, but the more they hear mathematical language, the more confident they will become at understanding it and, eventually, using it.

Key Vocabulary
forwards
backwards
remaining

If we add one more, how many do we have?

Questioning

Look out for speech bubbles below every objective to find examples of questions you can use to further develop your child's mathematical understanding. These are simply examples; you will come up with your own questions for your children. Questioning is a simple yet incredibly powerful technique to assess and extend your child's understanding. It distinguishes true understanding from simply memorising patterns and answers.

Online Support

While we firmly believe that mathematical concepts are best introduced through practical or visual examples, there are some excellent websites and apps available for additional practice. It is our recommendation that you use these sites alongside this book, to best support and challenge your child's developing maths skills.

MathShed

MathShed is a website and app used by many schools (and Blossom Home Education) to support pupils' development of mathematics by allowing them to practise at home, between lessons. MathShed games offer questions for every objective within the National Curriculum, separated by stage, for children working at reception to year 6 level. Questions are fun and varied and can be ordered according to difficulty, making this a very well-structured mathematics resource. While not free, subscriptions are extremely good value for money and a worthwhile investment!

Find MathShed here: www.mathshed.com

Top Marks

Top Marks is a free website, featuring a collection of games. While not organised by NC year group, they are grouped into categories and many fun games and interactive resources can be found here! We encourage you to explore this website when approaching new objectives, to offer your child a range of approaches to develop their skills!

Find Top Marks here: www.topmarks.co.uk

Blossom Home Education

While we heartily recommend the websites above, we cannot leave out our own version of online support! Blossom Home Education offers recorded online courses in Mathematics, for a very reasonable price. Many families (both home educating and school) purchase our courses to receive detailed video tutorials that support the current National Curriculum objectives. Used alongside practical activities and further practice from the websites above, this is an excellent blended learning solution.

Find us here: www.blossomhomeeducation.co.uk

Recommended Resources

Throughout this book, various resources are recommended, with explanations given. It is not compulsory to purchase any resources in order to follow the curriculum; these are simply recommendations. Neither the author nor Blossom Educational Publishing has been commissioned to recommend any of the resources in this book. They have been chosen for their suitability and brilliance!

All resources are available through Amazon and also listed on our website, www.blossomhomeeducation.co.uk.

Counters

It is hugely beneficial to use counters when approaching many of the objectives in this book. Use colourful, pleasing objects to excite your child, such as marbles or buttons or vary the counters you use, as I have done in this book. Dried pasta and beans work very well! Make sure the counters are available for your child to access, as their independence develops.

Numicon

Numicon is a hugely versatile resource that can be used to support so many of the learning objectives in this book. It is a worthwhile investment, as it continues to be useful as children advance through the curriculum.

The word mark Numicon is a registered trade mark owned by OUP. OUP is the publisher of the Numicon series of products, which can be accessed here: https://global.oup.com//education/content/primary/series/numicon/?region=uk

Base Ten Blocks

Base Ten Blocks, created by Learning Resources, are enormously beneficial in the teaching of mathematics at this stage and several years beyond. For the understanding of place value, this resource is invaluable.

Abacus

Ancient, yet still relevant in the teaching of mathematics, an abacus is a very useful counting tool, which many children enjoy playing with. In future years, it can be used to aid the learning of times tables. At this stage, the concepts of addition, subtraction, multiplication and division are made clearer with an abacus.

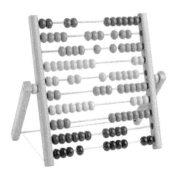

Balance Scales

These balance scales from Learning Resources are great fun for maths investigations. Use with Numicon to investigate number problems and compare the weight of different objects and substances. These are extremely popular with Blossom's 1:1 pupils!

Cubes

Cubes are great as counters and also very useful for measuring, before a child begins to use standard units.

Teaching Clock

Teaching clocks are great for demonstrating different times to your child and for them to see how the hands move in sequence with each other. This particular teaching clock, made by Learning Resources, is excellent, as the hour hand moves with the minute hand.

3D Shapes

To fully understand the properties of 3D shapes, your child is at a huge advantage if they have shapes to hold and examine. These shapes from Learning Resources are conveniently small and children enjoy sorting and playing with them.

Calendar

A calendar that you can adjust each day with your child is very helpful in developing your child's understanding of days, weeks, months and years. This one was made by Fridge Magic and we think it's great!

Analogue Clock

Displaying a clock, like this one, takes the stress away from learning to tell the time. Regularly referring to the clock will encourage your child's desire to learn and develop their understanding, without pressure. This colourful design, with silent movements, is one that many children would love to display in their room.

Number
and
Place Value

Arguably the most important objectives in this book, a child's understanding of number and place value forms a basis for most areas of mathematics. These skills should be taught explicitly and alongside other units, across the year.

Count to and cross 100, forwards and backwards, beginning with 0 or from any given number

When first learning to count, a child might be able to recite numbers in order long before they are able to count objects. When counting objects, you might notice that they lose their place, miss some out or count some more than once! This is a skill which requires practice but can be easily rehearsed using a range of everyday items and simple games.

Can you show me 15 marbles?

How many marbles do you have?

Key Vocabulary
forwards
backwards
remaining

At the beginning of Year 1, your child might still be learning to count up to 10 or 20 objects. Make sure they are confident in counting to and across 10, forwards and backwards, before moving onto higher numbers. **It is advisable to focus on 1-10, 1-20, 1-50, then 1-100, only moving onto the next stage once your child is ready.**

This can be taught explicitly, using objects like marbles and counters, but also in everyday life. Can your child count how many people are in the room? Can your child count how many biscuits are left in the jar?

You might find- at the start of Year 1- that your child does not yet recognise numbers greater than 10. That skill will develop across the year.

1, 2, 3,———, 5, 6, 7

13, 14, 15,——— ,17

25, 24, 23,——— , 21, 20

56, 57, 58,____ , 59, 60

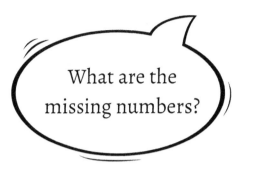

What are the missing numbers?

Use Numicon to assist counting numbers larger than 10. Before your child has grasped counting in tens, they can count the holes in the Numicon to work out the number!

Count, read and write numbers to 100 in numerals; count in multiples of twos, fives and tens

Key Vocabulary
odd
even
pattern

There are so many opportunities to read numbers! Plenty of board games and everyday items display numbers under 100. Sticker book collections are fantastic for this; children get so excited to collect stickers. Every time they get a new pack/sticker, they need to try to read the number, then match it to the same number in the sticker book! Model how to read the number, then ask them to try the next one!

Counting in multiples forms the basis of your child's first times-tables, which they will learn next year. Some children find it easy to learn to count in multiples by rote; this can mean that the objective is achieved sooner; however, learning by rote doesn't always indicate an understanding of the process of counting in multiples. Being able to count in fives, but not understanding that five is being added each time can present difficulties in subsequent years, when learning times tables.

A practical or pictoral approach is recommended, in addition to learning by rote, in order to give your child a deeper understanding of multiples.

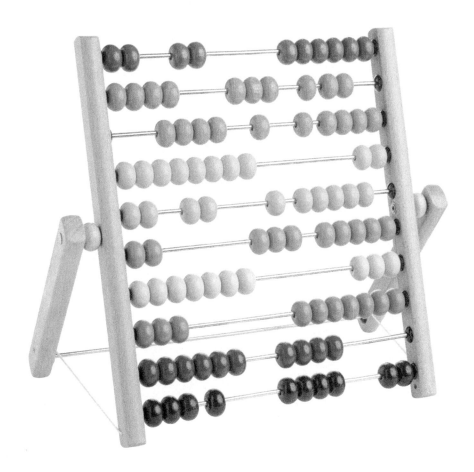

Numicon is a fantastic resource to use when beginning to count in multiples. Another method for counting in multiples is to group together small objects, like marbles, counters or even dried pasta/beans!

An abacus is a fantastic tool for developing counting skills and is a great investment for your home, much loved by mathematicians across time!

Given a number, identify one more and one less

If your child picked up counting easily and has been counting to ten or twenty for several years now, it might seem surprising to if they find it tricky to add or subtract one from a number.

The majority of children learn to count by rote: walking up the stairs and counting as they go; singing counting songs; counting with their families in the car. Learning by rote has its place; it allows children to learn to count before they have an understanding of number and place value. To develop this understanding further, practical activities are recommended.

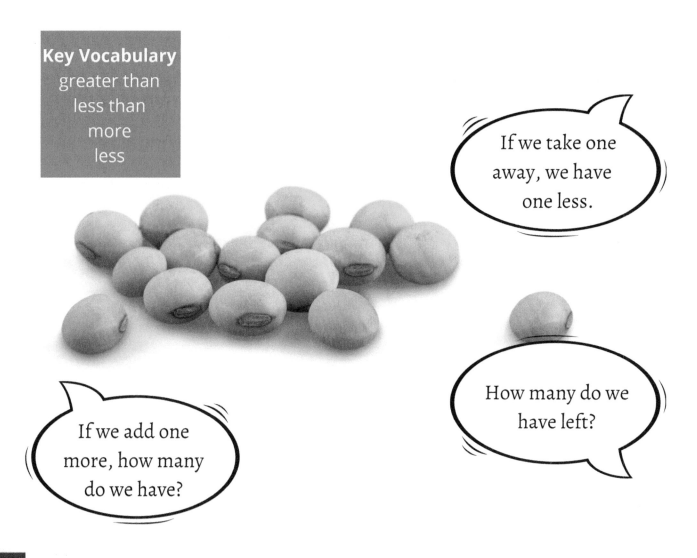

Key Vocabulary
greater than
less than
more
less

If we take one away, we have one less.

How many do we have left?

If we add one more, how many do we have?

The key to understanding this objective is language. Does your child know what 'one more' and 'one less' means? Consciously use this language during your everyday activities.

A number line is an excellent tool to aid this objective. Seeing the numbers in front of them allows your child to focus on the task set, without having to picture those numbers in their mind at the same time.

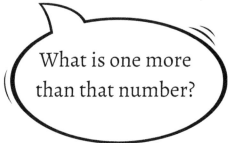

What is one more than that number?

By creating your own number line, together, you'll see how well your child understands number and have fun at the same time! Allow them to place the numbers in order, while you support and congratulate! Try 1-10 first, then move onto 1-20, then beyond!

0 1 2 3 4 5 6 7 8 9 10 11 12 13 14 15 16 17 18 19 20

Yes, well done! 5 is one more than 4 and 4 is one less than 5!

Keep your number line to use for future activities. Or, even better, display your number line and regularly refer to it, to build your child's number confidence!

Identify and represent numbers using objects and pictorial representations, including the number line and use the language of: equal to, more than, less than (fewer), most and least

This objective really tests your child's deeper understanding of place value, showing to what extent they understand the relationship between numbers and the formation of two-digit numbers.

Counting in multiples of ten, a previous objective, will be used and developed alongside this objective, as children learn to form two-digit numbers using objects and pictures.

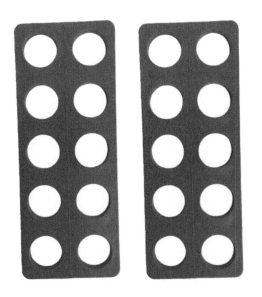

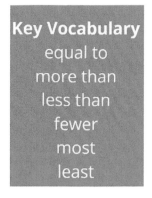

Key Vocabulary
equal to
more than
less than
fewer
most
least

Numicon is an example of a resource that can be used to clearly represent numbers. Use the tens with smaller numbers to create two-digit numbers.

Base Ten Blocks are extremely effective in tackling this objective, and many others! These resources allow children to see clearly that ten is equal to ten ones. These tools are an excellent investment into your child's Mathematics education, as they are beneficial to so many objectives, across years 1-6.

When your child learns to draw pictorial representations of numbers, they gain an independence as a learner, which will be invaluable to their future development. 'Drawing numbers' will allow them to add, subtract, multiply and divide before learning formal methods.

17

First pictorial representations might only represent ones. This is a valid starting point and demonstrates a child's counting skills.

Below, the pictorial representations of two-digit numbers use lines to show tens and small squares to represent ones. This is a common pictorial representation of numbers, used in schools and assessments, and works incredibly well alongside Base Ten Blocks.

34

72

Read and write numbers from 1 to 20 in numerals and words

This objective involves both literacy and mathematics skills. Learning to write individual numerals can be a challenge for some children and often numbers will be written backwards or unclearly for some time. Just like when children learn to form letters, it is useful to take a practical approach and to keep things fun!

Use a range of materials to create the shape of the number: playdough, bubbles on the side of the bath, marbles, counters, lego, string.

Key Vocabulary
numbers one to twenty

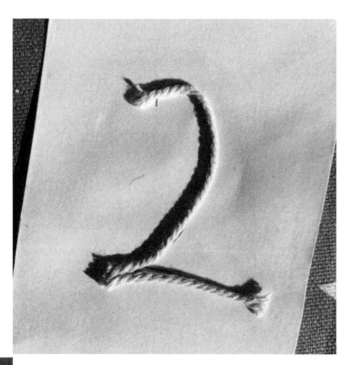

Draw the number in the air, with chalk on the pavement or with water on the fence.

If there is a number that your child finds difficult to draw accurately, creating some sensory resources can help, like this '2' shown glued onto card in string. Encourage your child to feel the shape of the number regularly before writing.

Two-digit numbers can be tricky to write, even when a child is able to form numerals correctly. Remembering which digit comes first becomes much easier once a child understands the composition of a number.

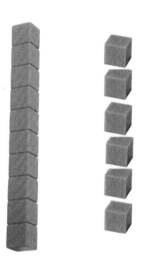

Sixteen can easily be written as sixty-one, until a child understands that the tens digit comes first, then the ones digit. They need to understand that eighteen contains one ten and eight ones, so must be written in that order. Base Ten Blocks can help with this!

Two-digit numbers can be tricky to write, even when a child is able to form numerals correctly. Remembering which digit comes first becomes much easier once a child understands the composition of a number.

eight	2
thirteen	13
nineteen	8
two	19

Ask your child to match the numeral to the correct word. Regularly show them the words for numbers or display these around the house, so they become familiar with them. Some of these words are quite tricky to read!

Once they can recognise and read these words, start practising how to spell them, using letter tiles and coloured pens to keep learning fun!

Number: Addition and Subtraction

Read, write and interpret mathematical statements involving addition, subtraction and equals signs

Key Vocabulary
add
plus
take away
subtract
total
altogether
equals

Before a child will successfully be able to understand the symbols for addition and subtraction, they need to understand what these terms mean. Use practical resources to demonstrate these functions, alongside the language.

Use any kind of counters, cubes or even your child's normal toys to demonstrate addition and subtraction.

Insert the new language into this activity once your child is gaining confidence. 2 cars, add 3 cars equals.... Demonstrate and repeat. Can they create their own addition sentence using their toys?

Begin to show your child how to represent this on paper, using pictures to help at first.

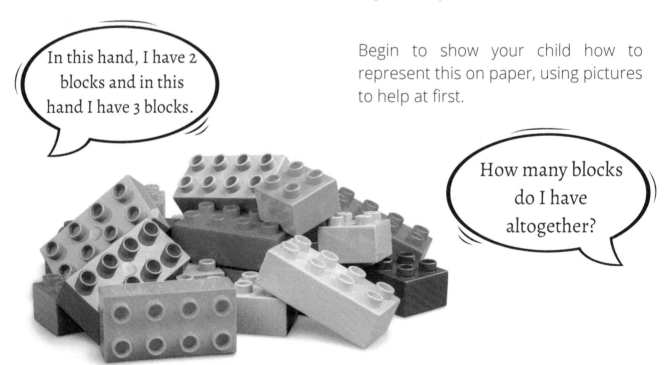

Repeat these activities for subtraction. It's normal for children to find this more challenging than addition, so you might need to spend longer on practical demonstrations. Introduce new language as your child gains confidence.

Part-whole models, like the ones below, can help your child to understand the meanings of addition and subtraction and to grasp the link between these two functions. Begin practically, then draw the numbers, then write the numerals.

I have 5 unicorns. I take one away. How many do I have left?

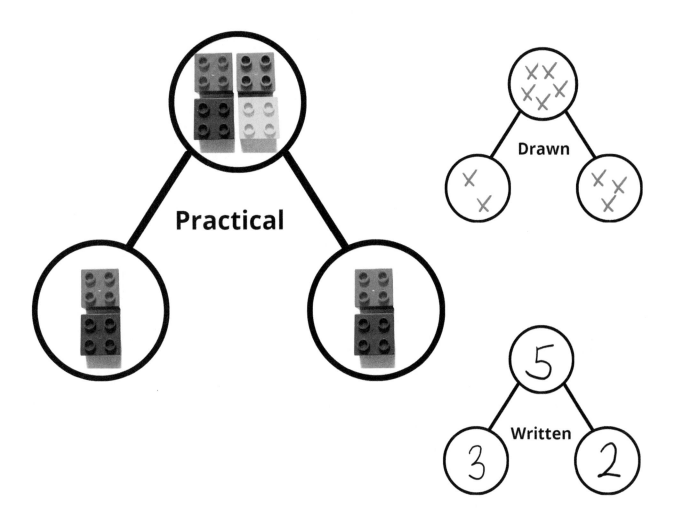

Practical

Drawn

Written

Represent and use number bonds and related subtraction facts within 20

The term 'number bonds' refers to simple addition calculations, which can be recognised and recalled quickly. In particular, knowing the numbers that can be added together to make 10 allows a child to approach a wider range of mathematical challenges more confidently in the future. As the above objective states, the aim at this stage is to build on those skills to recall addition and subtraction facts up to 20.

It is possible that your child can already recall their number bonds to 5. If not, this is a good place to start. Once they can recall that 5 can be made using 1 and 4, 2 and 3, 4 and 1 and 5 and 0, they will be ready to learn thier number bonds to 10.

Put down 2 fingers. How many fingers are left?

Some children like to think of number bonds as 'best friends': 6 is best friends with 4, 3 is best friends with 7, etc.

Get messy with finger paints! Paint 3 fingers yellow and the rest red. How many are red?

The best tools for learning number bonds are right in front of us!

Some children are excellent at learning 'by rote'. Their memory skills have developed enough to learn number facts by reciting them aloud or writing them down repeatedly until they remember. Whether or not this is the case, by investigating number bonds practically, their understanding will deepen and prepare them for future mathematical goals..

Numicon is a wonderful resource to use when investigating number bonds. Put the ten-shape onto a surface. Place another number on top. Can we find a number to fit over the rest to make ten?

Scatter Numicon shapes on a table. Create little puzzles, putting the shapes in pairs to make 10!

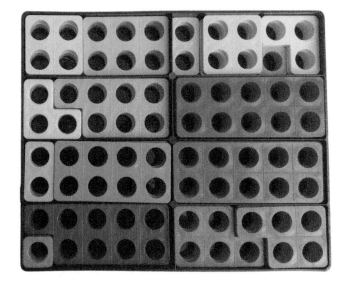

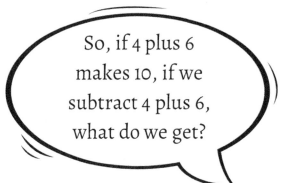

Don't forget to discuss subtraction facts alongside addition. It is normal for children to recal addition facts first, but subtraction becomes easier when the links with addition are discussed regularly. Whiile using a range of vocabulary, demonstrate adding and subtracting using practical tools, such as Numicon and counters, to solidify the understanding of these terms.

Another benefit to using Numicon is that it's perfectly weighted! Use Numicon with balance scales to develop an understanding of the term 'equal to'.

Put the ten-shape on one side and the three-shape on the other side of the scales. Investigate how to make the scales balance. What must be added to the three-shape?

One side holds a ten and the other side holds three.

How can we make the scales balance?

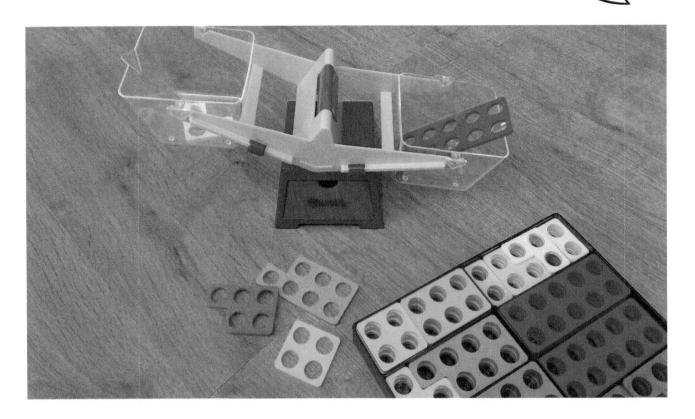

Once your child has a good knowledge of number bonds to 10 (addition and subtraction facts), move them onto higher numbers. Investigate making 20 using practical resources, such as Base 10 or Numicon.

Once they have put Numicon into pairs or used Base Ten Blocks to make 10, ask them how to turn 10 into 20. Once they have worked out that they need to add 10 to each pair, look carefully together at how they've made 20. Part-whole models, as shown below, can be useful to display their findings.

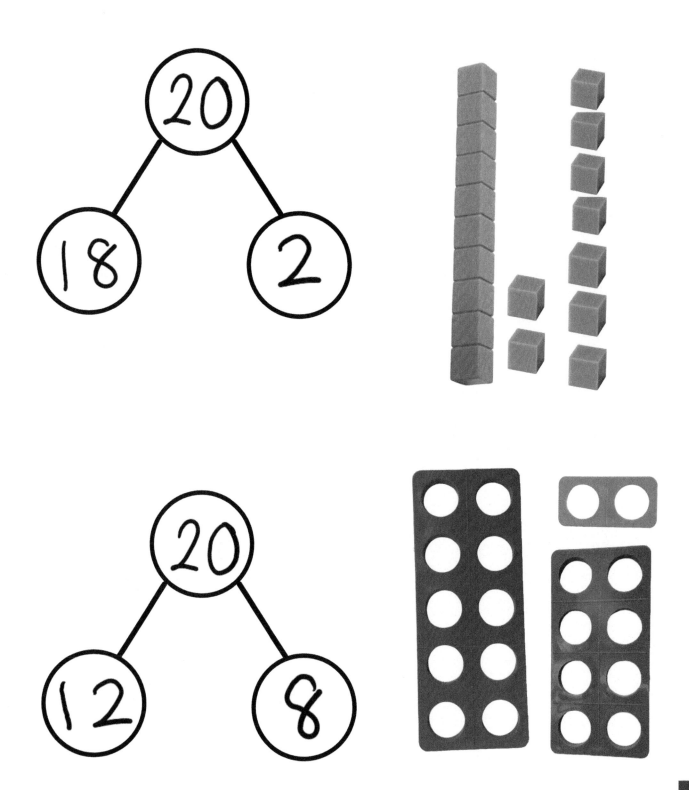

Add and subtract one-digit and two-digit numbers to 20, including zero

This objective links strongly to the previous objective based on number bonds, but-instead of remembering number facts- involves using strategies to add and subtract mentally and on paper.

0 1 2 3 4 5 6 7 8 9 10 11 12 13 14 15 16 17 18 19 20

A number line is a great way for children to add and subtract at this stage. These are available to purchase or alternatively can be printed from home or hand-drawn! It is a good idea to have some paper number lines available for your child to draw on when adding and subrtacting, as demonstrated below.

5 + 4

0 1 2 3 4 5 6 7 8 9 10 11 12 13 14 15 16 17 18 19 20

Watch carefully when your child begins using a number line. If they get the answer incorrect, what has gone wrong? It might be a counting error or perhaps they're starting at the wrong point.

Your child might be keen to just use their fingers when adding and subtracting. This is absolutely fine to continue, but it might become trickier to keep count when the answer is larger than 10.

Your child might be at a stage where they can add and subtract mentally, up to a point. Encourage them to use their knowledge of number bonds to help with their addition and subtraction. Numicon or counters could be used to help with this.

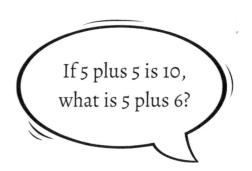

If 5 plus 5 is 10, what is 5 plus 6?

It becomes more difficult to add and subtract when needing to cross 10. As mentioned previously, children who use their fingers to assist them can lose count. Also, moving onto 2-digit numbers adds an extra level of challenge.

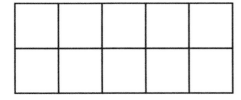

This diagram is called a tens frame. These can be bought, found on search engines and printed or created at home. Many children find these useful in developing their mental addition and subtraction when crossing 10.

Use the tens frames with practical resources, or print out several and allow children to draw on them.

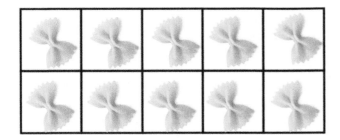
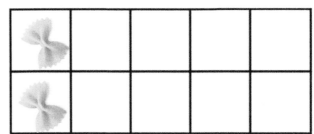

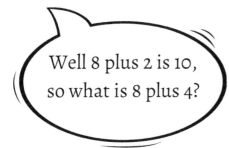

Well 8 plus 2 is 10, so what is 8 plus 4?

For this calculation, allow your child to put the 8 counters onto the first tens frame. Discuss that there are 2 squares left to get to 10, but that we have 4 counters to add.

Solve one-step problems that involve addition and subtraction, using concrete objects and pictorial representations, and missing number problems

Applying mathematical skills to real-life problems can often be found more challenging by children and adults alike. For this reason, it is encouraged to approach this objective continuously, alongside the rest of the objectives within this unit. Keeping problem solving separate to simple arithmetic can create unnecessary anxiety around this area of mathematics and delay progress.

Problems can be given verbally or written down for a child, depending on their reading age and confidence. Have a range of tools available for your child to select when working out problems.

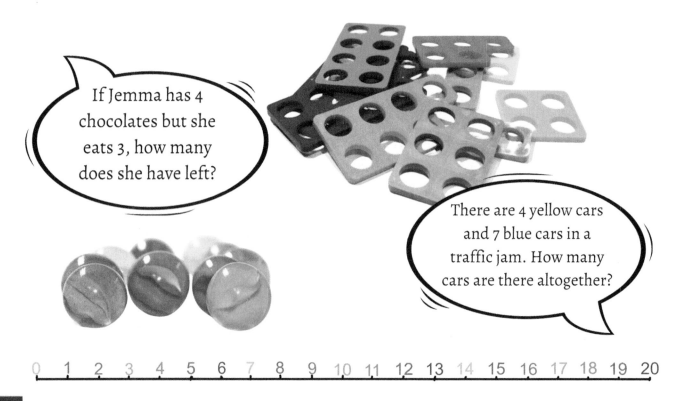

If Jemma has 4 chocolates but she eats 3, how many does she have left?

There are 4 yellow cars and 7 blue cars in a traffic jam. How many cars are there altogether?

0 1 2 3 4 5 6 7 8 9 10 11 12 13 14 15 16 17 18 19 20

Missing number problems are often a child's first experience of algebra! Sometimes, it can be surprising to learn that a child struggles with missing number problems, when the straightforward calculations are simple for them. Use sticky notes or toys to cover up the numbers. Practical resources, such as counters, could be used to work these out. If your child isn't keen on these straight away, work with them to develop strategies to work these out.

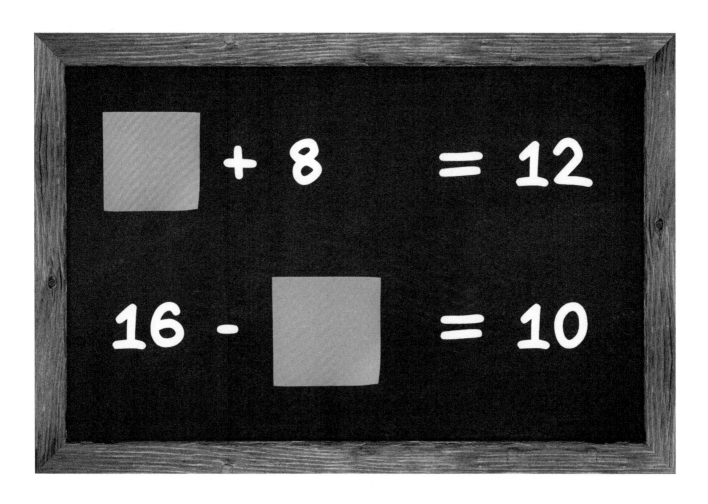

Something plus 8 is 12. Hold 8 marbles. How many more do you need make 12?

Number: Multiplication and Division

Solve one-step problems involving multiplication and division, by calculating the answer using concrete objects, pictorial representations and arrays with adult support

At this stage, it is useful for children to develop strategies to multiply and divide, although these terms might be new to them. The focus of this objective is to understand what multiplication and division is; rather than learning answers by rote, the emphasis must be on the language and the processes of multiplying and dividing.

Key Vocabulary
groups of
rows of
columns of
multiply by
share by
divide by
times
arrays

Can you put the buttons into three groups of two? How many are there altogether?

Use concrete objects to group objects, before moving onto pictorial representations. Build up their vocabulary in this area, beginning with language with which they are already confident. Develop your child's understanding of multiplication by relating it to addition.

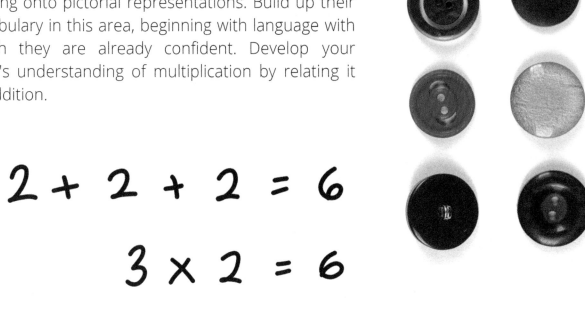

$$2 + 2 + 2 = 6$$

$$3 \times 2 = 6$$

How could we draw this?

Here we have three groups of two. This is two plus two plus two OR we can say three times two!

An **array** is arrangement of objects or drawings in rows or columns. This is a very useful method of investigating multiplication, as it is simple and clear.

Some children can find it tempting to draw elaborate pictures of their favourite animal or cartoon when drawing arrays! It's best to encourage them to stick to simple shapes in this case, so they don't forget the purpose of the drawing!

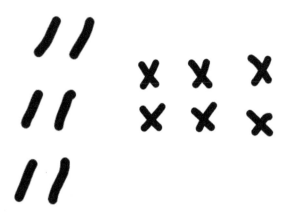

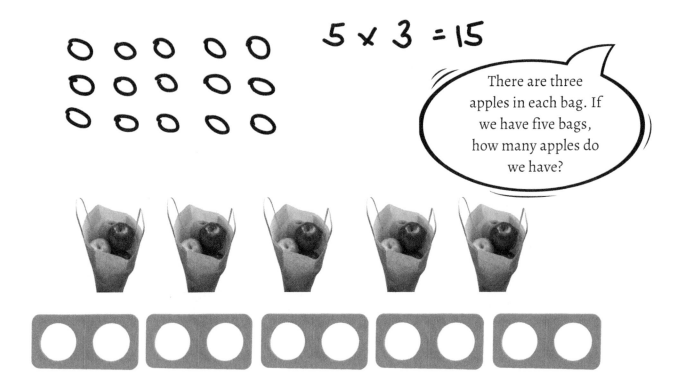

$5 \times 3 = 15$

There are three apples in each bag. If we have five bags, how many apples do we have?

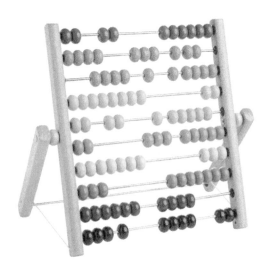

Although it is not a statutory requirement at this stage, it is strongly encouraged that children learn to count in 2s, 5s and 10s. This prepares them to learn these times tables next year, but also saves them time when counting groups/rows of these numbers of objects.

Demonstrate this using a number line or abacus to help! Help them to remember these numbers by singing/counting regularly together!

0 1 2 3 4 5 6 7 8 9 10

Perhaps your child has a favourite collectable toy, which they could use to practise creating arrays or counting in 2s, 5s or 10s?

Most children find division more difficult than multiplication. Similar practical and pictorial methods to multiplication can be used to develop understanding.

To introduce division, begin by describing it as 'sharing equally'. Using food might help to make this fun and demonstrate this new concept! You could even make this a family activity and use real people!

We have 6 sweets to share between 3 people. How many do they each get?

Share them out one at a time. One for you, one for you, one for you…

Once they understand how to work this out practically, demonstrate drawn methods. By drawing out rings for the number they're dividing by and sharing out the correct number of marks, they'll find the answer!

Share out 10 cookies between 2 plates. How many are on each plate?

Even if they know the answer straight away, encourage your child to practise the method of sharing items one at a time.

Number: Fractions

Recognise, find and name a half as one of two equal parts of an object, shape or quantity

At this stage, most children will be familiar with the term 'half' but might not have used it mathematically before. They also might not realise that the two halves of the same number or object are equal; it is not merely breaking something into two randomly sized pieces.

Ask your child to show half by drawing lines down the centre of shapes or colouring. Also, ask them to draw lines down the centre of a number of drawings, separating them into two groups.

Key Vocabulary
half
halve
whole
equal parts
double
share

Draw a straight line to show half of the cars.

Colour half of the petals yellow and half of the petals red.

Your child might have already learnt that some numbers have half the value of others. It is time to go over their prior knowledge of these and help them to learn more doubles and halves.

Numicon can be used very effectively to assess your child's understanding of the terms 'double' and 'half'. Firstly, present them with all the even numbers for this task. Demonstrate how two fours can fit on top of the eight. So half of eight is four and double four is eight. Then, look at all of the odd numbers: put two sevens together and count up how many holes there are in total.

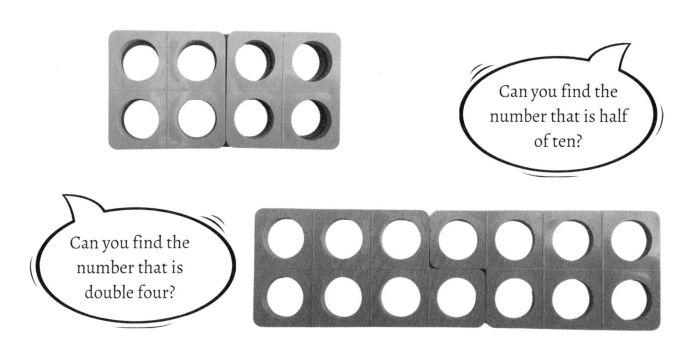

Use beads or counters to investigate more doubles and halves. Once they understand **how** to find doubles and halves, they can investigate by drawing. Do they understand that finding half is **sharing** by two? By linking the two objectives (halving and dividing), a child's mathematical understanding of these processes will deepen.

It's unlikely that your child has encountered half in its written form by this stage. It's a good idea to introduce that now, alongside the practical demonstration, but take special care to use a range of language to help them understand why it is written like this. At the moment, children aren't expected to learn the terms 'numerator' and 'denominator', but you might choose to introduce them if you think your child is ready.

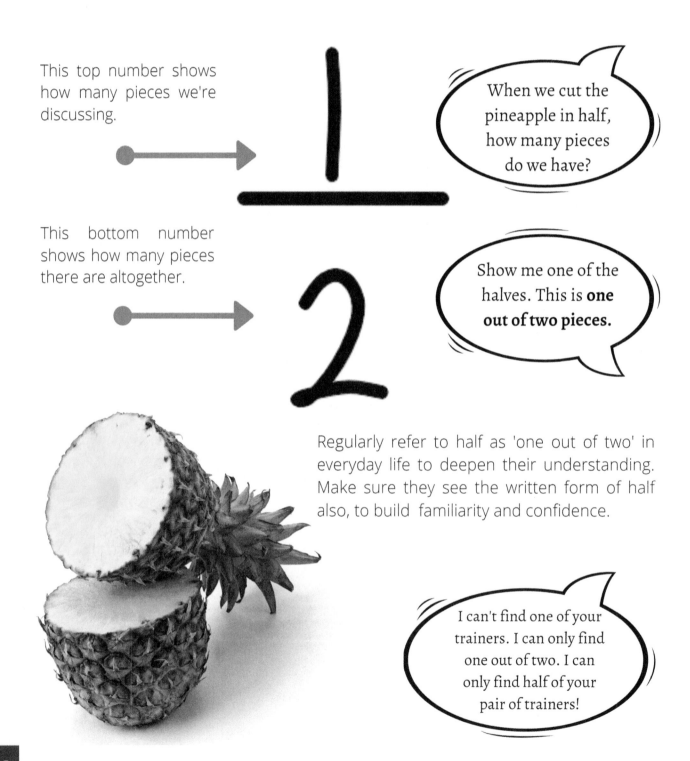

This top number shows how many pieces we're discussing.

This bottom number shows how many pieces there are altogether.

When we cut the pineapple in half, how many pieces do we have?

Show me one of the halves. This is **one out of two pieces.**

Regularly refer to half as 'one out of two' in everyday life to deepen their understanding. Make sure they see the written form of half also, to build familiarity and confidence.

I can't find one of your trainers. I can only find one out of two. I can only find half of your pair of trainers!

Recognise, find and name a quarter as one of four equal parts of an object, shape or quantity

After introducing halves, introduce quarters to your child. This might be another term with which they are already familiar, although they are less likely to have an understanding of what a quarter is. Use the same techniques to develop your child's understanding.

Demonstrate that when something is cut into four pieces, each piece is called one quarter. If you've already demonstrated how to write half as one over two, discuss with your child how to write one quarter, two quarters, three quarters and four quarters.

Key Vocabulary
quarter
share
fraction
equal parts
greater than
less than

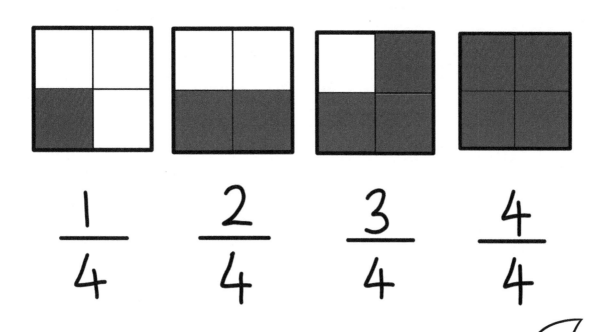

They might recognise that 2/4 is equal to 1/2. Encourage this and ask them to compare quarters and halves.

If four quarters has been shaded, the whole shape has been shaded.

Use coloured paper or card to create fraction puzzles! This simple activity is effective for developing fraction skills with children of all ages!

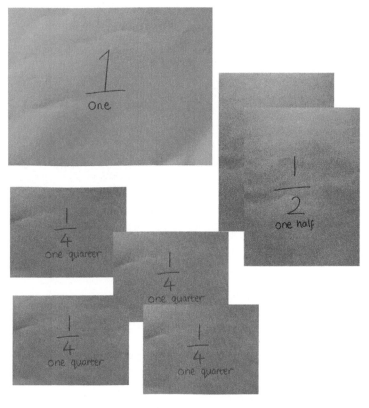

1. Take three sheets of paper, in different colours, if possible.
2. Write a big 1 on one sheet. You could also write 'one whole'.
3. Together, fold and cut another colour into two equally sized pieces. Discuss that there are now two pieces. Each piece is one out of two. Label each half as shown.
4. Together, fold and cut another colour into four equally sized pieces. Discuss that there are now four pieces. Each piece is one out of four. Label as shown.

> How many quarters are the same size as one whole?

> What is greater, one half or three quarters?

> How many quarters are the same size as one half?

If your child is confident with this, you might choose to move them on. Create another sheet of quarters, in the same colour. Demonstrate that 5/4 is greater than one and investigate how many quarters there are in 2! This goes beyond this stage, but is a worthwhile extension when a child is ready.

Measurement

Compare, describe and solve practical problems for the length and height

These objectives involve using clear vocabulary to compare the size of objects. Investigation is at the heart of this topic: make predictions, play and discuss. The more you model this language, the easier it will be for your child to pick it up. It is likely that they already use some of this vocabulary. These activities will allow you to assess how accurately they use it and to extend them effectively.

Key Vocabulary
taller
longer
shorter
equal
shortest
longest
tallest
in order

Can you draw a boy and a girl who are equal in height?

The boy is **taller** than the girl.
The girl is **shorter** than the boy.

Tell me about your toy trucks. Which one is longer? Which one is taller? Which one is shorter?

Let's put your toys in order of shortest to longest.

Challenge your child to tell you which pencil is the longest. Have they noticed that the pencils are not lined up correctly? Demonstrate how to line them up to compare accurately.

You might notice that your child has a good understanding of this but isn't currently using the language correctly. They might say things like 'the car is short than the truck'. Encourage them by modelling the correct language regularly and they'll soon pick it up!

Measure and begin to record lengths and heights

Measuring and recording is a topic that can be really simple to fit into everyday activities. Before measuring using standard units, start by measuring using non-standard units, such as cubes and straws, as shown below. Make sure your child understands how to line the objects up correctly for accuracy.

Key Vocabulary
measure
record
length
height
long
wide
width
tall
greater than
less than

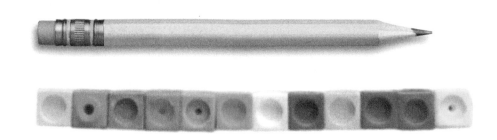

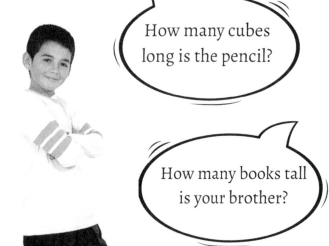

How many cubes long is the pencil?

How many books tall is your brother?

There are many objects that can be used as non-standard units. Consider using objects that interest your child.

The second part of this objective is to record their measurements. Depending on your child's writing ability at this stage, you might decide to write the words down for them and ask them to fill in the gaps, as shown below.

Mummy is _____ dinosaurs tall.

Next, your child needs to use their understanding of measure so far to measure using standard units. At school, they're likely to use centimetres before other units and might soon move onto metres

A fun activity could be to find lots of different units using rules, tape measures and height charts. At this stage, they don't need to worry about conversions, although you might feel that your child is ready to investigate these!

How tall is your dolls house? How wide is it?

Measure both of your trains. Which has the greater width?

Use the comparison language to solve problems involving measure, as shown previously within this unit.

Compare, describe and solve practical problems for mass or weight

Have fun exploring weight/mass with your child. Allow them to hold different objects in their hands and discuss which feels heavier. Balance scales, like these shown below, are great fun and an effective way to develop an interest in exploring weight/mass.

Key Vocabulary
heavier
lighter
equal to
heaviest
lightest

Are larger objects always heavier? Let's find out!

Alternatively, you could enjoy creating your own 'balance scales' or compare your own weights using a seesaw at the park!

Which side of the scales do you think will go down? Why?

Measure and begin to record mass/weight

When beginning to measure mass/weight with your child, use non-standard units such as multilink cubes or (for heavier objects) wooden blocks with balance scales. After practical investigations, look at pictures of balance scales, like the illustations shown at the bottom of this page.

Key Vocabulary
measure
weigh
weight
mass
balance
equal to
greater than
less than

Would it be better to use the small cubes or the large wooden blocks to measure the object?

Measurement

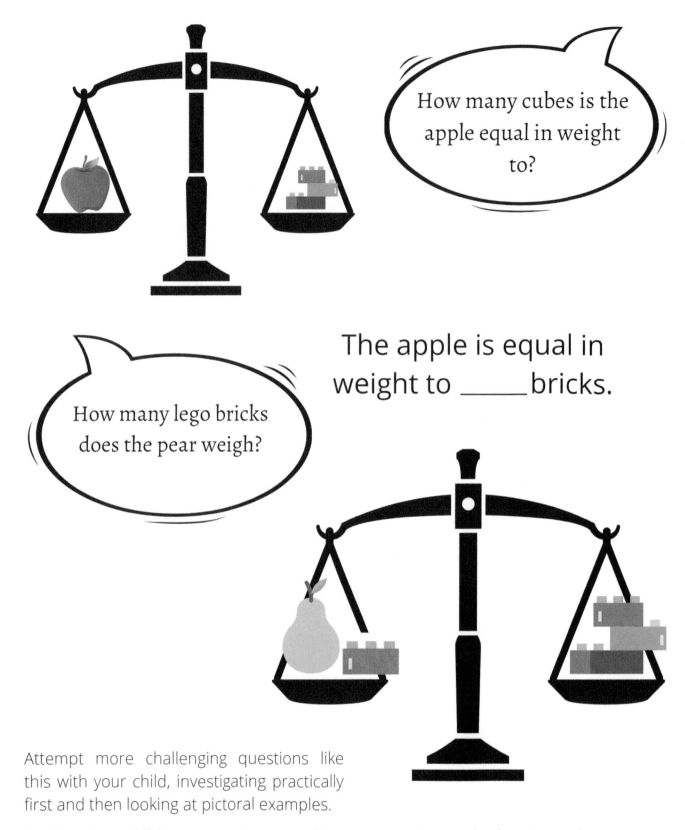

At this stage, children are not expected to measure in standard units, such as grams. That doesn't mean that you can't begin using them with your own child, but it's important not to skip the stage described in this unit, as your child needs to develop an understanding of meaning of weight and mass.

Compare, describe and solve practical problems for capacity and volume

Introduce the concept of capacity being the amount that something can hold and volume being the amount of space that an object occupies or holds. Children are not expected to be able to recite these meanings, but it's useful for them to have an understanding so that they can compare two volumes or capacities.

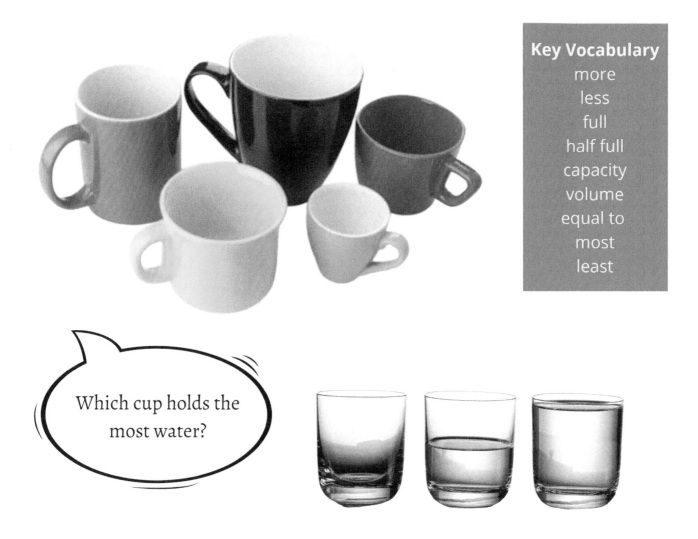

Key Vocabulary
more
less
full
half full
capacity
volume
equal to
most
least

Which cup holds the most water?

Ask your child to demonstrate filling, half filling and leaving other containers empty, using liquids or sand. Prompt them to use the language listed above when describing how full containers are.

Measure and begin to record capacity and volume

At this stage, children are expected to measure non-standard unit containers using non-standard unit objects. In simple terms, how many of one object can fit in another?

The ___ has a capacity of ___ _____ .

	1	2	3	4
	5			

Introduce a table as a means of displaying data. Can they work out the rest of the answers by noticing a pattern? Drawing or discussing might help with this!

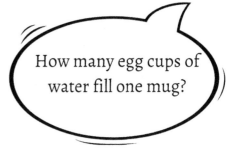

How many egg cups of water fill one mug?

Investigate using liquids and different sized containers!

If three egg cups of water fill one cup and five cups of water fill one jug, how many egg cups of water will fill one jug?

Create investigations like this for your child to explore measuring capacity. Use objects that vary in size and shape. Many children will forget to fill containers completely when measuring, which causes inaccuracies. A fun way to approach this is to make the error yourself and ask your child to tell you what you did wrong!

Compare, describe and solve practical problems for time

Solving time problems does not always involve a clock. Within this stage, your child develops their use of time language, progresses their understanding of days, months and years and also builds on their ability to tell the time.

Over the next few pages, there are many ideas for comparing, describing and solving practical problems for time. It is best to make these part of daily conversations, in order to embed new learning fully.

Some objectives, such as recalling the days of the week, might already be familiar to your child. In fact, some early talkers will learn to recite the days of the week as young toddlers. But to understand deeply, they need to be able to apply this knowledge to problem solving.

Key Vocabulary
before
after
first
next
then
now
finally
today
tomorrow
yesterday
(days of the week)
(months of the year)

It is my birthday tomorrow!

Today is Tuesday. On what day will it be my birthday?

Allow your child to play with stopwatches and timers, using them for practical activities like cooking and simply to experiment. Becoming familiar with the role that time plays in real life will encourage their enthusiasm.

Sequence events in chronological order using language

   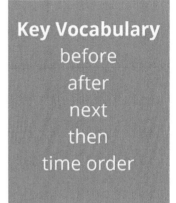

Before I filled the glass, it was empty.

After I filled the glass, it was full.

Next, I drank some water and the glass was half full.

Key Vocabulary
before
after
next
then
time order

Create short stories with your child, using pictures to show the time order of events. You could even link this to the stories they like reading with you and discuss what happens first, next and finally. Also, use this language when discussing activities they enjoy.

Before we go to Grandma's house, what do we need to do?

Recognise and use language relating to dates, including days of the week, months and years

If your child if not yet able to recall the days of the week, encourage this by displaying the date each morning. You could write this or buy/create a calendar to use together. If they already know the days of the week and months of the year, discuss these regularly to assess and extend their understanding.

This magnetic calendar from Fridge Magic is a perfect example of a simple resource to develop your child's understanding of days and months.

Key Vocabulary
days of the week
months of the year
date
yesterday
today
tomorrow
timetable
how many

> Yesterday was Wednesday, so what day is it tomorrow?

Create a visual timetable for the week, showing them which activities occur on each day. Can they read the timetable themselves and answer questions about their week?

> What day do you have football practice? How many days is that from now?

Children can learn the order of the days of the week and months of the year in the same way they learn to count. Normally these are learnt by rote, by reciting them like song lyrics. Make sure they understand the order fully by asking questions and having discussions about what happens each day and each month.

Measure and begin to record time (hours, minutes and seconds)

Does your child know which is longer: an hour a minute or a second? They might do, by this stage or they might not! This objective involves developing an understanding of how long each unit of time represents. Sand timers can be very useful to help with this, as can stopwatches and analogue clocks.

Key Vocabulary
hours
minutes
seconds
less than
greater than
time
measure

How many goals can you score in one minute?

How long does it take to write your name three times?

Develop your child's understanding of hours, minutes and seconds by asking them which is the most appropriate for measuring different activities. We wouldn't measure a football match in seconds or measure the duration of a song in hours.

Tell the time to the hour and half past the hour and draw the hands on a clock face to show these times

Learning to tell the time is something that simply must be taught at home. Even when a child attends school, the packed maths curriculum means that there just isn't enough time for most children to learn how to tell the time. It is a subject which needs to be taught and practised regularly, as part of everyday life.

Key Vocabulary
O'Clock
Half past
later than
earlier than
minute hand
hour hand
time
clock

For many children, learning to tell the time is extremely difficult. Many families only have digital clocks in their houses and their children find it hard to understand an analogue clock. It is really useful to display the time in your home using an analogue clock, as well as digital. The wall clock shown below, with bright colours and clear numbers is a great example of a clock that will help your child. If possible, display the time in their bedroom and in communal areas and regularly refer to it when discussing plans.

At this stage, children are expected to learn to tell the time to the hour and half past the hour. Only move them further than this if you feel they're confident in this area.

Teaching clocks, like this example above, are really useful for teaching children to tell the time. The best ones are those that are linked so that the hour-hand moves when the minute-hand is pushed round.

Playing games like 'What's the Time Mr Wolf?' can take the pressure off and make your child feel more at ease with telling the time. Adapt this game by asking them to create the time on a teaching clock or asking them to read the time when you make it on a teaching clock.

Another fun activity is for them to make their own clock, like this one!

FInd printable versions of blank clock faces online, to use with your child. Can they draw the hands in the correct places or match complete clock faces to the correct times?

What time is it? Can you show this time on your clock?

If your child picks this up quickly, you can move them onto more times past the hour. The second half of the clock is normally more challenging to grasp.

Remember that your child will pick these skills up in their own time, as long as they are given regular opportunities to practise. Simply putting a clock on the wall and referring to it regularly will spark your child's interest and engage them in wanting to develop this important skill, without pressure.

Recognise and know the value of different denominations of coins and notes

Key Vocabulary
penny
pound
coin
note
(all types of coins and notes)
sort
value
greater than
less than

By this age, many children are able to recognise certain coins and notes and have some understanding of the values. However, in the age of online shopping, debit card transactions and 'Apple Pay', children today are naturally less familiar with money than previous generations. At this stage, it is important for children to learn the value of different denominations of coins and notes and to begin to count using money.

Find the number on the coin. Which coin has the lowest number?

Please may you sort these coins out for me, so that all the matching coins are together?

Plastic (toy) coins can be purchased, but many families find that it works better to collect spare change gradually and use that with their children. Ask for their help in sorting the coins and prompt them to read the numbers and words displayed on the front of the coin.

It is common for children to expect the larger coins to have higher values. Once they have mastered the pence, show them £1 and £2 coins. Explain that £1 has the value of 100 pennies!

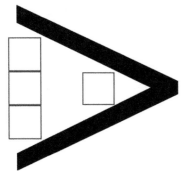

Use the greater than and lesser than symbols to see if your child understands the values of the coins. Help them to understand the symbol by showing how a greater number of cubes will fit at the open end!

Once they recognise and understand the value of coins, introduce them to notes. Practise using the same methods that your child has enjoyed.

I have a silver coin in my hand. It's worth more than 5p but less than 20p. What must it be?

You might prefer to print out photos of notes!

69

Measurement

Setting up a shop for your children, using coins from your loose change pot, can really inspire their development in this area.

You can also visit actual shops, of course, and let your child help to find the correct money when paying!

The soup costs 50p. Can we make 50p from the coins you have left?

Give your children different combinations of coins and ask them to work out the total. In addition to this, ask them to create different totals using the coins they have. This can link very well with counting in 2s, 5s and 10s.

You have four 10p coins. Do you have enough to buy a 50p chocolate bar?

Geometry: Properties of Shapes

Recognise and name common 2D and 3D shapes

Your child might already know some names of 2D and 3D shapes, or this could be an area in need of great focus. The curriculum is non-specific when it comes to the shapes they should name, so this is something you and your child can lead. It is a good idea to begin with the shapes below, before moving onto shapes with more sides.

Cut out and display pictures of different shapes and ask your child to sort them into groups. Rather than memorise using flashcards or learning by rote, your child might prefer to learn the names of shapes using games, like bingo, or by chatting to you while cutting shapes out of playdough. Go on a shape hunt around your house and see how many of different shapes you can find!

Do you like the square I've made? Can you cut out a square too?

Lolly sticks are fantastic for creating shapes. Using simple resources like these or straws will bring out the creativity in your child and allow them to explore 2D shape fully!

Key Vocabulary
names of 2D and 3D shapes
sides
edges
faces
corners
more
less

To learn 3D shapes, it is hugely beneficial for your child to have access to handheld resources, like those shown below. Learning these shapes by simply looking at pictures is less likely to give your child a deep understanding of the difference between 2D and 3D shapes. Playing with and examining solid shapes will allow your child's curiosity to lead their learning, encouraged by your questioning!

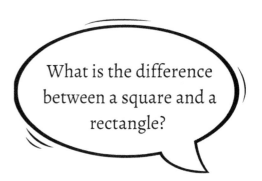

What is the difference between a square and a rectangle?

Here is a fun game to play with the shapes below:

How many faces does a cube have? What shape is each face?

- Hand out the shapes so that you each have the same five shapes in front of you (E.g. a sphere, a cone, a cube, a cuboid and a square-based pyramid), hidden from each other's view.
- Put one of your shapes under a cup in the middle of the table.
- They have to work out which one you have chosen by looking at their own shapes and asking questions. E.g. How many faces does it have?

Make patterns with 2D and 3D shapes. Use the correct terminology when discussing the patterns to develop your child's understanding.

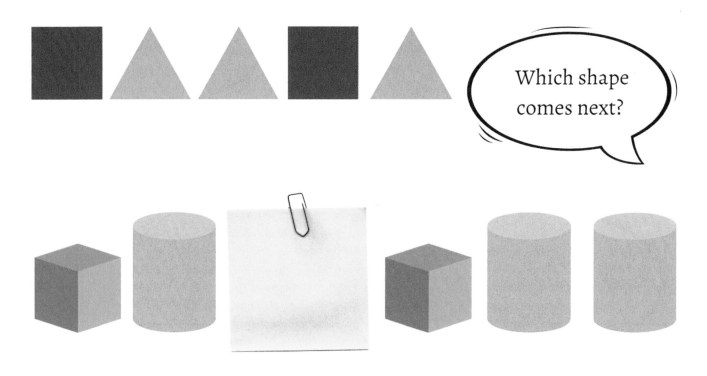

The possibilities are endless when it comes to creating patterns with shapes. Allow your child to paint, draw print and carve to create repetitive, sequential patterns to extend their understanding of shape.

Purchasing some stencils will help your child to accurately draw 3D shapes, which might encourage them to create some lovely patterns! Remember to always call the shapes by their correct names to develop their understanding.

Geometry: Position and Direction

Describe position, directions and movements, including whole, half, quarter and three-quarter turns

This objective requires the child to describe the rotation of a person, shape or object. The vocabulary clearly links to their understanding of fractions, but some children find it more challenging to use that language when discussing position.

It can be fun to practise positioning by asking your child to stand and turn! First, ask them to make a full turn. Then ask if they can make just half a turn. If this goes well, ask them to make a quarter turn, followed by a three quarter turn. You could also play this game using a teddy bear or toy!

Make a full turn.

Make a half turn.

Who will the bear be facing if he makes a half turn?

Key Vocabulary
full turn
half turn
quarter turn
three quarter turn
rotate
forwards
backwards
left
right
top
bottom
above
below
in between

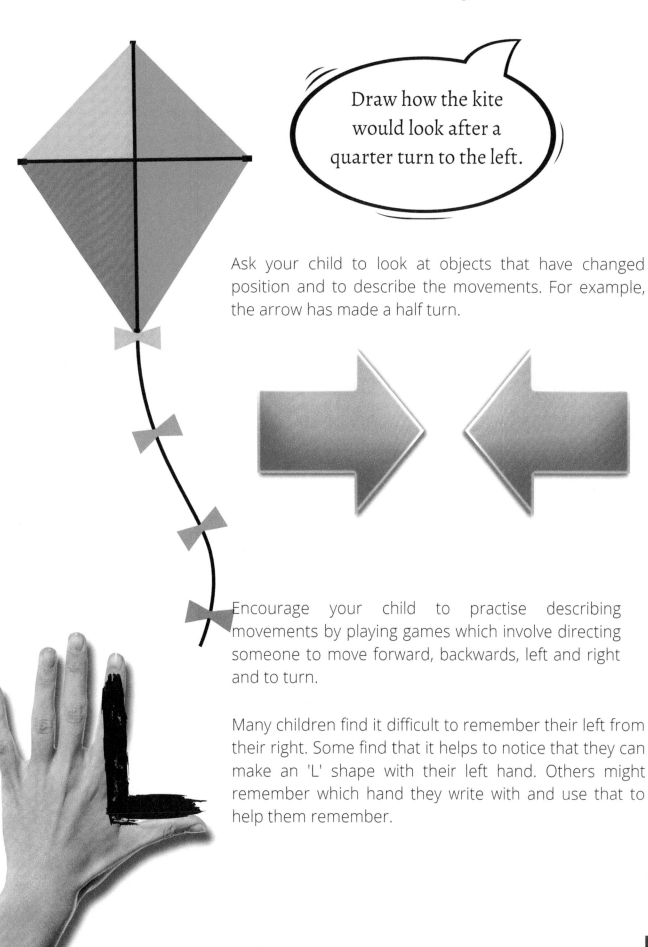

Draw how the kite would look after a quarter turn to the left.

Ask your child to look at objects that have changed position and to describe the movements. For example, the arrow has made a half turn.

Encourage your child to practise describing movements by playing games which involve directing someone to move forward, backwards, left and right and to turn.

Many children find it difficult to remember their left from their right. Some find that it helps to notice that they can make an 'L' shape with their left hand. Others might remember which hand they write with and use that to help them remember.

77

Ask your child to describe the position of objects in relation to each other. Use toys or objects that they are familiar with and turn this into a game!

The kangeroo is to the left of the panda. Which animal is behind the lion?

Ask your child to describe the position of objects in relation to each other. Use toys or objects that they are familiar with and turn this into a game!

Can you put a toy in between the doll and the football?

The doll is to the right of the football.

We really hope this book has been useful to your family in supporting your home education journey. We would love to hear how you are getting on and to see photos of your home maths activities.

Get in touch or tag us on social media!

www.facebook.com/blossomhomeeducation

www.instagram.com/blossomhomeed

www.instagram.com/blossom_educational_publishing

www.twitter.com/blossom_homeed

Join our friendly group for parents, for more tips and advice on supporting your child's learning at home:

www.facebook.com/blossomeducationalsupport

Printed in Great Britain
by Amazon